Saturday
SCHOOL

**How One Town
Kept Out
"The Jewish,"
1902-1932**

I have read somewhere, in Dionysius of Halicarnassus, I think, that History is philosophy teaching by example.

Henry St. John Bolingbroke (1678 -1751)
On the Study and Use of History, Letter 2

Saturday
SCHOOL

**How One Town
Kept Out
"The Jewish,"
1902-1932**

by
Tom Keating

Phi Delta Kappa Educational Foundation
Bloomington, Indiana U.S.A.

Cover design by
Victoria Voelker

Phi Delta Kappa Educational Foundation
408 North Union Street
Post Office Box 789
Bloomington, Indiana 47402-0789
U.S.A.

Printed in the United States of America

Library of Congress Catalog Card Number 99-70216
ISBN 0-87367-813-3
Copyright © 1999 by Tom Keating

For Lynne

Acknowledgments

I wish to thank, first and foremost, all the individuals who spoke with me during personal and telephone interviews and conversations. From the Square Table Restaurant to the Library of Congress, each person has been helpful.

My gratitude extends to my editors, Donovan R. Walling and David Ruetschlin, and to professor Thomas Head for his thorough critique.

My appreciation continues to the helpful personnel of the Monroe C. Gutman Library at the Graduate School of Education of Harvard University, Special Collections Room of the Decatur Library, Special Collections of the Woodruff Library at Emory University, Library of Congress, DeKalb Historical Society, American and Southern Jewish Historical Societies, Jewish Community Archives of Atlanta, Chautauqua Institution Archives, Atlanta History Center, City of Decatur, and especially City Schools of Decatur.

I am grateful to the Metro Atlanta Chapter and District VII of Phi Delta Kappa International for emotional and financial support in the early stages of this effort.

Finally, I humbly thank our son, Jeff, who taught me to accept other's attitudes toward difference; Stephanie, our daughter, who helped me to distinguish between "special" and "different"; and especially Lynne, my wife, who exemplifies how to love each person without regard to difference.

Table of Contents

Chapter 1
School on Saturday 1

Chapter 2
Meetings and Motions 5

Chapter 3
A History of Inconvenience 15

Chapter 4
Seven Possibilities and an Answer 21

Chapter 5
Decatur: Homes, Schools, Churches, and a Junkyard . . . 31

Chapter 6
A Parallel Case 43

Chapter 7
What's True? Who Cares? 47

Appendix 51

Bibliography 57

About the Author 59

Table of Illustrations

pages 7-13   The photographs of Charles D. McKinney (p. 7), George Scott Candler (p. 8), Lamar Ferguson (p. 10), and Mrs. William Schley Howard (p. 14) are taken from an official photograph of the Decatur Board of Education, circa 1937. The photograph is used courtesy of the Decatur Public Library Special Collections.

page 26   R.C.W. Ramspeck, circa 1929. Photograph is from the Archives of the DeKalb Historical Society, used with permission.

pages 32-33   The map of the original corporate limits of the town of Decatur, Georgia, is from the collection of the DeKalb Historical Society, used with permission.

page 52   Lynne Keating at the Monroe C. Gutman Library at the Graduate School of Education of Harvard University in 1995. Photograph by Tom Keating.

1

School on Saturday

From 1902 until 1932 the public schools in Decatur, Georgia, held classes on Saturday and used Monday as the weekly school holiday. A number of reasons have been put forward for this peculiar practice, but the one that resounds most strongly is that a powerful group of Decatur citizens contrived to perpetuate the practice in order to discourage Jews from settling in the town. This informal history tells the story of how one town's leading citizens covertly worked to keep out "the Jewish" over a 30-year period.

It is appropriate to take up this story in the 1920s. On Tuesday, 8 March 1927, the six-person Board of Education of Decatur, Georgia, recorded a tie vote on whether to continue having the schools' weekly holiday on Monday instead of Saturday (Board of Education, *Minutes*, 1920-1929). It was a bitterly divisive issue, and the board required a roll call ballot with board members' names printed in the minutes. The vote was a tie, and Decatur's peculiar, 25-year practice of having school on Saturdays was continued for five more years.

To this day, no one has told the story of Saturday school in Decatur or explained the hidden agenda that created and sustained this tradition. The purpose of this monograph is to do precisely that: to share the story of why Decatur had school on Saturdays and not on Mondays. Many, perhaps most, of the facts and issues are being made public for the first time.

Unfortunately, the histories of local public schools often are recounted as administrative litanies. They recite the names of principals and other administrators or recount the exaggerated heroics of certain superintendents. Many of us have spent a large part of our pre-adult years in a public school, yet most of us tell our stories about public education through the symbols of reunions, with yearbook pictures and remembered sports championships. Yes, it is important to record who was principal and when; but it is even more critical to write about who was principal and *why*. The firing of a principal, the burning of a school, and the loss of accreditation —these things do not happen in a vacuum. Public education history is more than administrative gloss.

Because public education is a pivotal institution in our culture, the issues surrounding Decatur's school week are entwined with other issues during the first third of the 20th century. But the history of Decatur's school week also is shrouded in misleading discussions about "policy."

To make policy means to allocate or make choices among limited resources. Making policy also allows the policy makers to control the agenda of the schools and, to some extent, to control discussion. Once a school board has set a policy, then administrators can use that policy to foreclose discussion. Administrators often refer to policy as an ultimate authority; because a policy exists, things must be done just so. Thus school leaders reify policy, making it a thing separate from their own decisions. For those school leaders, policy becomes either a shield or a weapon.

In Decatur during the first third of the 20th century, policy was a weapon designed to exclude certain students from school. A few powerful men successfully kept a whole group of children out of school by using an exceedingly subtle method, the school calendar.

Decatur's policy of holding school on Saturdays instead of Mondays illustrates dramatically the gap that so often falls between rhetoric and reality. We say as an article of faith that public education is the great equalizer, that it is open to all, that we welcome all the poor and the rich, the literate and the illiterate, the native and the naturalized, the athlete and the academic. The unfortunate reality is that too often students have been excluded for wholly arbitrary reasons.

The story of Decatur's exclusionary policies might have gone untold had it not been for an octogenarian woman who wanted to tell her own history of the public schools she attended. Frances Freeborn Pauley, a 1923 graduate of Decatur High School, first mentioned the fact of Decatur's contrivance in late winter of 1991 while she was lobbying for Georgia poverty victims. As she and I stood discussing public education on the marble steps of the Georgia state capitol, she asked me if I knew that Decatur once had Saturday classes and a weekly Monday holiday. She mentioned several possible reasons, and I mentally filed away the information. But it began to fascinate me. Thus I embarked on three years of intensive research to learn more about real public school histories, with all their awkward truths, uncertainties, and complexities.

The Saturday school practice was designed partly in public meetings through the use of motions taken by the school board. As is still so often the case, ordinary, often seemingly boring, meetings hold the key to understanding actions by public bodies such as school boards. In Decatur, Georgia, five meetings dealt with Saturday school. We shall begin with the two most dramatic: a meeting on 8 February 1927 and, one month later, the recorded vote on March 8.

2

Meetings and Motions

The 8 February 1927 school board meeting began a month of debate, acrimony, and division in Decatur. Not since the founding of the public school system, which prevailed in 1901 by only a single vote, had Decatur experienced such a contentious education issue (Board of Education, *Minutes,* 1920-1929).

New Year's in 1927 had come in the usual way. In line with the established custom, classes had resumed on Tuesday, 4 January 1927, following the 16-day Christmas holiday. Decatur students always began the new year on Tuesdays, and 1927 was no exception. The yearbook, the *Caveat Emptor,* noted the prevailing atti tude: "Back to the greasy grind." A fortnight later, as they did every year on January 19, the high school students assembled in chapel for programs commemorating the birthday of Robert E. Lee. Seven days later the semester ended. Students continued their classes but would not congregate in chapel again until a month later, when they would assemble for the yearly commemorative speeches celebrating George Washington's birthday on Tuesday, 22 February 1927.

The board of education met at its usual time, 7:30 p.m. on the second Tuesday of the month, February 8. They met at their usual location, in the superintendent's office (Board of Education, *Minutes,* 1920-1929). While the setting, time, and place seemed unexceptional, the event proved historic.

One board member was not at that meeting; George Scott Candler was vacationing in Clearwater, Florida. Three sets of minutes were read, which took only a few moments. Former Superintendent Glausier spoke concerning a student's diploma, without action being taken by the board. Then the next four sentences of the official minutes hinted at the drama of the Saturday school issue. Those sentences are:

> Several ladies of the city, accompanied by Mr. Doughman and Mr. Freeborne [sic], presented a petition requesting the Board to change the school holiday from Monday to Saturday; and Mrs. Campbell was present to oppose the attempt. After hearing both sides, the Board agreed upon motion of Mrs. Hoke, to vote on the matter at its next regular meeting. In the meantime, upon motion of Dr. Hopkins, the Superintendent was instructed to send a colorless questionnaire to all patrons of the schools to ascertain their wishes for the information of the Board. Drs. Hopkins and Sledd were to cooperate in this. (Board of Education, *Minutes*, 1920-1929)

The unnamed ladies likely included members of the PTA Saturday Holiday Committee. The men were stalwarts of the community. Frank A. Doughman was an attorney practicing at 19 Edgewood Avenue, a short streetcar ride away in Atlanta. W.W. Freeborn had become a city commissioner a year before and, during his eight-year tenure, would rise to become *mayor pro tempore*. Another supporter of the movement for a Saturday holiday was William Schley Howard. Howard was a former U.S. congressman and a prominent lawyer. His wife, Lucia Augusta duVinage Howard, founded the Decatur Recreation Board and would serve on the Decatur School Board for almost two decades. The Howards lived on West College Avenue.

Mrs. J.A. Campbell was no stranger to public issues in the community. She was married to John Alton Campbell, a bookkeeper who worked in Atlanta and who served for a few months on the newly formed City Commission in 1922. John Campbell was part of the *en masse*, yet amicable, resignation of the 1922 city commission, an action that led to the ascendency of George Scott Candler as a city, county, and regional power. Now Mrs. Campbell stood with those who favored keeping the peculiar practice of a Monday holiday. The Campbells lived on South McDonough.

The members of the 1927 board of education who favored the Saturday holiday were:

Charles D. McKinney

First, Charles D. McKinney, age 54. McKinney resided on South McDonough. In 1927, McKinney headed his own mortgage and investment company. A Presbyterian and a stalwart proponent of public education, McKinney regularly served as chairman of the Board of Education.

Second, Catherine Hoke, age 52. Hoke resided at 103 Hood Circle. Her husband, John, was a mechanical engineer. Catherine Hoke was the only woman appointed to the board. Early in her tenure, she had expressed interest in changing the holiday.

Third, Dr. Frank T. Hopkins, age 52. Hopkins, a dentist, registered a key vote each time the holiday issue became public.

The equally strong opponents of change were:

First, George Scott Candler, age 39. A lawyer by training, Candler was a civic leader. In 1927 he was the mayor and an ex-offico member of the school board. Candler was a Presbyterian. He also was a war hero and the Decatur scion of the Murphy-Candler families.

Second, Andrew Sledd, Ph.D., age 56. Sledd lived in the Great Lakes area of Decatur. He was a professor of Bible studies at

George Scott Chandler

Emory University and the father of seven children. Sledd was the secretary of the board of education, though in 1924 a PTA-sponsored petition was circulated that opposed his re-appointment because, among other reasons, he made "caustic remarks about our school teachers and public school."

Third, Homer B. Adams, age 58. Adams was involved in real estate. He lived at 506 Clairmont avenue with his wife, Marguerite, and their daughter. Adams had been appointed to the board in 1922 to fill the position left open when George Scott Candler became Decatur's mayor. Adams and Sledd were members of the First Methodist Church.

Members of the board of education were appointed to six-year terms by the City Commission. It would be interesting to know just how the commission selected the appointees. Regrettably, no extant documents nor insights from the interviews cast much light on the appointments from 1922 to 1927. It is known that in 1927 Commissioner Freeborn and former Commissioner Howard would have favored change and that Mayor Candler strongly opposed altering the Saturday school schedule.

One often-repeated story that circulated until the late 1970s was that Decatur's school board had seats for Prebyterians, Methodists, and Baptists. This religious/civic connection probably was much stronger in the 1920s, though that remains to be studied. Also needing more study is the connection between the Presbyterian Church, Agnes Scott College, and the mayoral tenure of George Scott Candler.

However, the connection between the churches and local politics is illustrated by a local anecdote about a colored person who came to Decatur and asked where Jesus' church was. A townsman responded that he knew where Frank Thomas' church was (Methodist), and he knew the location of Scott Candler's church (Presbyterian) and even Guy Rutland's church (Baptist). But no one in Decatur knew where Jesus' church was. The point of the fable is that powerful local men were associated with churches in Decatur; and they made sure their influence was citywide, not just limited to one congregation (Ridley, 11 April 1995).

The petition that was brought to the board on 8 February 1927 was signed by parents and others in the community who were willing to place themselves on record as wanting the weekly holiday changed from Monday to Saturday.

While both sides talked to the superintendent and board, no action was taken in February. The prominent Mr. Candler was absent, still on vacation in Florida with his wife and son, George Scott Jr. Candler's considerable personal influence and his official power as mayor meant that no decision would occur without him. So Mrs. Hoke moved and the board agreed to vote on the matter at the March meeting (Board of Education, *Minutes,* 1920-1929).

However, the next item in the minutes was something unusual. Dr. Hopkins moved and the board "instructed" the superintendent to send a "colorless questionnaire" to all patrons (Board of Education, *Minutes, 1920-1929)*. By today's standards, giving the chief executive a direct order may not seem unusual. But in the 1920s, when administrators had not acquired much prominence, the matter was hardly routine. In 1927 it was an unheard of exercise of legislative power for a board to direct the superintendent to survey the public, at least in Decatur. Such an order had the potential to lead to board-superintendent-community conflict. By surveying the public, the board was, in effect, placing the issue of Saturday school before the people in the first plebiscite in Decatur school board history.

9

We know from the official minutes that Drs. Hopkins and Sledd were told to cooperate with Superintendent Lamar Ferguson. Thus the board assured itself that representatives from both sides of the issue would help keep the proceedings fair.

Superintendent Lamar Ferguson

We also know from the March board records that the "colorless" questionnaire went to white families only. "Colorless" undoubtedly meant an unbiased set of questions. Thus in early March, Superintendent Ferguson sent 1,075 survey cards to white families in Decatur (Atlanta *Constitution*, 2 March 1927).

The Atlanta *Constitution* printed a 200-word article about the survey, with the headline, "Parents of Decatur to Vote on Change of School Holiday." According to the *Constitution*:

> Parents of Decatur school children will be asked this week to express their desires in regard to changing the school holiday from Monday to Saturday, according to announcement of Lamar Ferguson, superintendent of schools, who said that cards are being mailed to heads of 1,075 white families represented in the Decatur school system.
>
> These cards will be returned to the board of education and action will be taken on the proposed change at the next meeting which will be next Tuesday. Mr. Ferguson said the expressed desires of the parents will be used by the board in making a decision on the question and whatever decision is made will not take effect until the fall term of school.
>
> The move to change the weekly holiday was instigated recently at the last regular meeting of the board by William

Schley Howard as representative of the Parent Teacher bodies of Decatur. Parent-Teacher leaders are said to favor the change because athletic events in which pupils of the junior high schools take part are nearly all held on Saturday and Decatur students are not enabled to participate. Opponents of the change say that if Monday is made a regular school day it will force students to prepare their lessons on Sunday. (2 March 1927, p. 5)

It is interesting to note that the *Constitution* portrayed the question as just a matter of the details of schooling. Nowhere in the article is there a hint of the tremendous cultural and political split over the question of Saturday school, an issue that divided the board, patrons, school faculty, and even Decatur families.

On Thursday, 3 March 1927, the DeKalb *New Era* printed a letter from the PTA Saturday Holiday Committee. The 15-paragraph statement offered the committee's reasons for changing the school holiday from Monday to Saturday. The first reason offered was the same as that given in the *Constitution* article, that is, the conflict between Saturday school and athletics:

> All other schools that we meet in athletics have their holidays on Saturday. Our children must return to school the next day [Saturday] with lessons half prepared, or not attended at all.

Two other reasons associated with sports follow, then the PTA Saturday Holiday Committee used a subhead: "Either Change Our Holiday or Abandon Athletics." Then the committee presents a reason for changing the school schedule that, while still related to sports, also has an economic element:

> Saturday school interferes with the parents taking their children to inter-collegiate games in Atlanta. Many boys work at these games and either have to be excused from school early or do not come to school at all. The absentee list is normal on week days averaging 17 per cent. On Saurday it is increased to 47 per cent.

The next two reasons presented by the committee are related to social and family life:

All the entertainments and social affairs given in connection with the school must either be given on a school night or a Saturday night. This brings you to a Sabbath unprepared.

Many of our business men have Saturday half holiday, and if it were not for Saturday school, would be able to take their families on weekend trips. Fathers of boys see too little of them.

What follows seems at first just a bit of fabrication; but I think it was felt as truth seven decades ago. In addition, we must keep in mind the public controversy about motion pictures and the many issues that were raised over "decent" talking films.

All the advantages of the city are offered the children on Saturday, and our children are unable to avail themselves of them.

If you take your children to a motion picture show, is it not better to be able to take them to an educational one? A show that is sponsored by the P.T.A. and prepared especially for the children?

Saturday school in Decatur and Monday school in Atlanta has a tendency to separate families and relatives who live in the respective cities, [and] otherwise mix in a social way.

The PTA committee then moved from social to monetary issues:

All competitive meets in the Boy Scouts, Girl Scouts, Camp Fire and Girl Reserve organizations are held on Saturday. Our children cannot attend, or must be excused from school.

With Saturday holiday our business men would hire our boys for extra help on Friday afternoon and Saturday instead of sending into Atlanta as they now do. Many boys need this extra money in order that they may remain in school. There is practically no work to be secured on Monday. It is not altogether a matter of work. High school boys should be taught the value of work.

We are out of step with the rest of the country. Alabama even legislates against Saturday teaching. If Saturday is such a fine day for school, why do not other towns and cities adopt it?

From an economic standpoint, we are paying for five days of school and we get little more than three in the high school, and all our children eventually reach the high school. (DeKalb *New Era,* 3 March 1927, p. 8. Emphasis added)

The following Tuesday, March 8, the board voted on the question of Saturday school. The official minutes record a historic moment, a dramatic action, and an unprecedented decision by a board member. From the official minutes:

The question of the change of holiday from Monday to Saturday was then taken up and discussed; upon the demand of Mr. McKinney the vote was taken by poll, with the following results:

For Monday		For Saturday	
Popular Vote:	**Board:**	**Board:**	**Popular Vote:**
197	Adams	Mrs. Hoke	**413**
	Candler	Hopkins	
	Sledd	McKinney	

In view of the tie vote, the holiday remains as it is at present, on Monday. The Board then dajourned [sic]. (Board of Education, *Minutes,* 1920-1929)

The board president or superintendent presumably asked for an oral vote:

For changing the holiday from Monday to Saturday, a roll of the board will be called alphabetically: Adams, nay. Candler, nay. Hopkins, yea. Hoke, yea. McKinney, yea. Sledd, nay. (Board of Education, *Minutes,* 1920-1929)

The holiday remained Monday because of the parliamentary rule that a tie vote defeats a motion. The effects of this tie vote were to last another five years.

What had happened to Mr. Ferguson's statement in the *Constitution* that the express desires of the parents would be used by the board in making a decision? Approximately 1,000 families had received cards, presumably for one vote per family. More than 600, or six out of every 10 eligible patrons, had responded. A two-to-one majority was in favor of a Saturday holiday. Three board members reflected that popular majority sentiment. Mr. McKinney had resolutely demanded a roll call vote, a first in the annals of the City of Decatur Board of Education. Yet the change did not pass.

Mrs. William Schley Howard

That public vote affected the board itself almost immediately. Ten days later, Catherine Hoke resigned from the Board of Education with nine months remaining in her term. And just two months later, the City Commission appointed Mrs. William Schley Howard to fill her unexpired term (Board of Education, *Minutes*, 1920-1929; City Commission, *Minutes*, 4 January 1924 to 1 June 1928).

3

A History of
Inconvenience

The vote on 8 March 1927 may have been dramatic, but it did not come "out of the blue." In fact, the issue of Saturday school had simmered in the community since at least 1921, when Decatur still was officially a "town."

The superintendent hired before Ferguson, G.W. Glausier, had recognized early in his administration that having school on Saturday and a holiday on Monday was administratively cumbersome. Because of the peculiar practice of Saturday school, Decatur often had to adjust its schedules so that teachers could attend training days. In May 1921, for example, he recommended closing the schools on Friday and Saturday, May 6 and 7, so that teachers could attend the State Education Association meeting (Board of Education, *Minutes*, 1920-1929). His request contained the provision that Saturday's work should be made up by teaching on Monday, 2 May 1921.

The first official attempt to change the school schedule was made by Glausier and the board during the 1921 Thanksgiving week. On the Monday before Thanksgiving, the board of education met in Superintendent Glausier's office. Under the "New Business" agenda item was a proposal from the superintendent to change the weekly holiday from Monday to Saturday (Board of Education, *Minutes*, 1920-1929). As was frequently the case in the debates surrounding Saturday school, the question before the

15

board was not what day to have classes but what day should be the school holiday.

It is important to remember that during the first decades after the formation of school districts along modern administrative lines, the power of the school superintendent was not clearly defined. Today it is not only common for a superintendent to propose policy, it also is common in many small communities for the superintendent's recommendations to be quickly approved. In Decatur, whose school system had been authorized in 1889 and opened in 1902, the superintendent did not have such power.

However, Glausier's recommendation was quickly supported by Charles McKinney, a member of the board of education who had been a city commissioner when the public school system was founded. McKinney moved that the recommended change start at the beginning of the spring term (Board of Education, *Minutes*, 1920-1929).

Although Glausier's recommendation was supported with a motion by a respected board member, the motion was tabled until the next meeting on 13 December 1921 (Board of Education, *Minutes*, 1920-1929). The minutes are silent on who made the motion to table McKinney's motion and on who seconded the motion to table it. Instead, the board took an action that it took each year before the holidays:

> In regard to the Christmas holidays, the Superintendent was authorized to hold school on the Monday preceding Christmas Day and then to close for the holidays on Friday, December 23rd and reopen on Tuesday, January 9th, 1922. (Board of Education, *Minutes*, 1920-1929)

One interesting item illustrated by the quote above is that, because of having a Monday holiday, Decatur had to adjust its Thanksgiving and Christmas holiday schedule each year. In fact, at least three times each year the Board of Education had the opportunity to change the school schedule when its members had to officially approve the school calendar and officially change that calendar to accommodate holidays and teacher training days.

16

There is no official policy on the subject recorded in the minutes of either the Board of Education or the City Commission; thus the Board of Education was free to set the school calendar to meet the needs of the schools. However, the minutes of the board meetings that dealt with the school calendar do not include any mention of a reason for having school on Saturday.

Somewhat inexplicably, the minutes of the December 13 meeting do not show whether the question of the weekly holiday even came up. Though it is not uncommon for politicians to use delaying tactics against proposals they wish to defeat, the absence of a requested item from the agenda of a school board in the early 1920s does seem unusual. Apparently, instead of discussing the weekly schedule, the board again changed the schedule for the Christmas holiday. The new dates for the holiday were Saturday, 17 December 1921, to Tuesday, 3 January 1922 (Board of Education, *Minutes*, 1920-1929).

The minutes of that meeting do not explain what had prompted superintendent Glausier to suggest the change in the holiday. However, another political crisis was brewing in the town of Decatur. On 3 March 1922 the entire City Commission resigned in a controversy that split neighbors, townsfolk, and political allies (City Commission, *Minutes*, 3 January 1916 to 21 Dec. 1923). That controversy concerned the form the new city government would take; and it ended one month later, on 7 April 1922, when a new commission and mayor were chosen for the "City" of Decatur. George Scott Candler became mayor and an ex officio member of the board of education. By the summer of 1922, the political climate, the form of government, and the status of the town had changed dramatically.

Because Candler was now an ex officio member of the board of education by virtue of his position as mayor of Decatur, another member needed to be appointed to fill Candler's old position on the board. In May 1922, Homer B. Adams was appointed to fill that position (City Commission, *Minutes*, 3 January 1916 to 21 Dec. 1923).

The motion to change the weekly holiday was again before the Board of Education on 29 August 1922. At this meeting, for the

17

first time, the names of individual board members appear in the public record. According to these records, Candler moved to have the holiday remain on Monday. Andrew Sledd, who was the board secretary and had seen the second-longest service on the board, seconded the motion (Board of Education, *Minutes*, 1920-1929).

Candler and Sledd had managed to change the form of the question being considered. The earlier efforts had been to change the holiday. Now, the proponents of the status quo had moved to keep an established practice and to portray their opponents as somewhat revolutionary. And in the 1920s, being a revolutionary was not a particularly attractive or popular position.

In addition, by phrasing the question in terms of changing the school *holiday*, the focus was shifted away from the reasons for having school on a particular day and, in particular, the effect of having school on Saturday. Thus the Monday holiday could be considered as an established custom without having to consider the freakishness and inconvenience of having school on Saturday.

The motion, of course, would have received the two votes of Candler and Sledd. The minutes do not list the votes on this motion, but Hoke and McKinney, the earliest known board proponent of a Saturday holiday, must have voted "nay," because the board chairman was faced with a tie vote and Homer Adams was not at the meeting that night. According to the minutes:

> Upon a tie vote, the Chairman [Dr. F.T. Hopkins] cast the deciding vote in favor of the motions as stated. (Board of Education, *Minutes*, 1920-1929)

After Dr. Hopkins voted for the holiday to remain on Monday, he apparently felt the need to explain his vote. The board minutes contain the statement, ". . . and explained that he [Hopkins] so voted because he was convinced that Monday is an unsatisfactory school day." As an explanation, that statement is very unsatisfactory.

There are many unanswered questions concerning this vote. For example, why had the measure been delayed until August 1922 when it had been scheduled the previous December? And

18

when the measure finally reached the board, why was the ex officio member able to reformulate the question?

Why was Saturday school continued for so long, in spite of the fact that a survey in 1927 found that most white citizens would have preferred school to be held on Monday?

And, of course, the most basic question is, Why did Decatur have Saturday school in the first place?

These questions are not answered by the official records or newspaper articles of the day. In order to try to find the answer of why Decatur had Saturday school, I interviewed a number of older citizens who had been in the Decatur schools during the years when school was held on Saturday.

4

Seven Possibilities and an Answer

Decatur's peculiar practice of Saturday school and Monday holiday for its public schools raises several fundamental questions: Why? For what motive? Who benefited? Who lost out? Unfortunately, the answers found in the written records are unsatisfactory, at best.

In order to find an answer, I gathered an oral history. I conducted both formal and informal interviews with more than 30 people (see Appendix, *Interviews)* via phone and in person. The ages of the 16 persons interviewed in person ranged from the 70s to the 90s. They included seven females and nine males, and all except one were white. I interviewed 19 persons by telephone, including five females and 14 males. Their ages ranged from the 50s to the 80s. Some of those interviewed graduated from the Decatur schools in 1923, 1926, and 1932, when the Decatur schools held classes on Saturday.

All interviewees were asked if they knew about Saturday school and if they would describe their experiences. They also were asked to share any ideas about why Decatur had school on Saturday and a weekly holiday on Monday. Once the interviewees understood the nature of this public school history, they usually were willing to discuss what they remembered. Generally, the women interviewed were more forthright in their discussions.

After conducting the interviews, I listed the reasons proposed for Decatur's peculiar practice and grouped those reasons that

21

were similar. That produced a list of eight proposed reasons for having school on Saturday.

Many of those who offered reasons offered more than one or speculated about what others might think. Many of the interviewees concluded that they were not sure why Decatur had school on Saturday. Thus the reader should keep in mind that what follows is an accumulation and composite of research interviews.

The eight reasons proposed for having school on Saturday are:

1. Monday was washday.
2. The agricultural schedule demanded it.
3. Agnes Scott College students needed more time to return to campus.
4. Decatur was just different.
5. Circuit-riding ministers needed Monday as a travel or rest day.
6. Monday was an unsatisfactory school day.
7. It kept students from doing their homework on Sunday, the Christian day of worship.
8. It kept Jews out of Decatur because they worshipped on Saturday.

Monday was washday. An African-American woman was the first to suggest this reason during an informal telephone conversation. Later, two other black women mentioned the Monday washday as a reason for having school on Saturday. To find out more about this custom, I attended the annual barbecue of the Trinity-Herring School Alumni group on a sunny September Saturday. A large crowd of alumni had gathered to share stories of their school days. I met a woman in her late eighties who gave her name simply as Ms. Lula. She discussed washday in greater detail:

> Monday was washday. We went to the white folks' house and got the dirty washing. We'd start the wash on Monday and return it on Thursday or Friday. Then next Monday we'd begin all over. Of course Monday was washday. But we

went to school on Saturdays because Superintendent Ferguson said so. (Calloway, 6 September 1997)

On Mondays, black women and their children walked the
unpaved streets leading from the "colored" section, up a steep
hill, and through the center of town to Clairmont Road. Some
wealthier whites had their homes on Clairmont Road. The
women and children each returned with a basket of white shirts.

However, given the tenor of the times in Georgia, it is unlikely that the school district adopted so unusual a schedule because
it was more convenient for black women who took in laundry. It
is much more likely that black students attended school on Saturday because, as Ms. Lula explained, "Superintendent Ferguson
said so."

The agricultural schedule demanded it. Four interviewees al-
leged that Decatur had school on Saturday because farms required a long day of field work on Saturday and, therefore, a day
of rest following Sunday worship. Some interviewees talked
about farm families coming to town on Saturday to get supplies,
to socialize, and to take care of "city things."

Many communities throughout the United States did schedule
vacations and classes around the rotation of crops. However, if
the family farms needed Saturdays for work, then why have
school on that day? Why allow school to interfere with a basic
agricultural need? The agricultural reason fails to explain school
on Saturdays in Decatur.

Agnes Scott College students needed more time. Three people
suggested that Agnes Scott College students, who went home for
the weekend, did not get back until Monday; therefore they
needed that extra day for travel or rest. None of the interviewees
could explain how the needs of Agnes Scott students related to
the operation of a nearby public school.

Started as the Decatur Female Seminary in 1889, Agnes Scott
Institute, and later Agnes Scott College, was located in a wooded
lot between McDonough and Church Streets. Today it is located

on East College Avenue and is a leading women's liberal arts institution, as well as the leading higher education institution in Decatur.

There were definite connections between the Decatur Presbyterian Church and Agnes Scott College. The "Scotties" often were daughters of prominent citizens, and certainly most often the daughters of respected Protestant, especially Presbyterian, community members. But a cause-and-effect relationship between a travel day for female students and the peculiar practice of a weekly holiday on Monday seems very unlikely.

Decatur was just different. In the hearts of many old-timers in Decatur, a fourth reason is a completely credible explanation. It is simply that Decatur was somehow different. Indeed, the notion that Decatur *was* different, and *is* different, remains a standard belief to this day.

In the early part of this century, Decatur described itself as a Christian enclave and an ideal place made up of homes, schools, and churches. One of the stories told to me by several old-timers early in my research was that Decatur Presbyterians would stop wagons coming from the Appalachian mountains when they approached the town. "Are you Presbyterian?" a God-fearing Decaturite would ask. If the response was No, then the newly arrived were admonished to "Roll on." In addition, Decatur supposedly illustrated its difference by telling the railroad not to build a stop in the city.

> There is a well worn story that the people of Decatur would not allow the Georgia Railroad to locate its terminals here and for that reason the road had to be built six miles farther out in the woods; and hence the terminus located in what is now the heart of Atlanta. The more plausible version is that the necessary land could not be obtained in Decatur which was already an old and thickly settled town. (DeKalb *New Era*, 17 February 1927)

It is common for groups of people to describe themselves as different from others and therefore as special. In Decatur, that tendency was expressed mostly in separating the townspeople from those in Atlanta. For example, when discussing whether Decatur should allow movies to be shown on Sundays, R.C.W. Ramspeck, author of "Decaturgrams," a front-page column in the DeKalb *New Albany*, wrote:

> Decatur is different from even Atlanta on questions of this nature and we believe that this difference in itself accounts for a large part of the wonderful growth our city has had in recent years. Just because Atlanta does a certain thing is no reason for Decatur to follow. Individuality is often a great asset. (Thursday, 17 March 1927).

To stress individuality and difference and to tie that into the boosterism fever that applauds promiscuous growth and equates it with progress was not that exceptional, especially in the bally-hoo years of the 1920s. Indeed, Ramspeck stressed the difference between Decatur and Atlanta even more strongly in his column of 17 March 1927:

> Decatur and Atlanta should establish a line running north and south as a boundary for all time between the two cities. Atlanta should come no further east and Decatur should go no further west. It might be wise to make our line in the southwest portion of Decatur straight, giving Atlanta a small part of our territory. Decatur should have Emory University if it is to become part of either city. The officials of Emory prefer to come this way rather than in Atlanta, but the movement there has possibly gone too far now for this to take place. It would be well for our citizens to be thinking of city limits extension. The legislature meets this June and does not meet again for two years.

Ramspeck, and others, probably had other lines drawn in their minds. The established white Protestant majority drew many lines between themselves and the blacks, Jews, and Catholics. Ramspeck surely reflected his times and the thoughts of others in 1915 when he supported rechartering the Ku Klux Klan. His name appears as the only recognized DeKalb County personage on the formal rechartering documents filed in Fulton Superior Court, 26 April 1916 (p. 497), according to both the original, which I have seen, and the documents associated with the Hearings on the Ku Klux Klan before the House Committee on Rules of the U.S. Congress (Fogelson and Rubenstein 1969, p. 101).

R.C.W. Ramspeck

There is no doubt that Decatur was clannish, even Klannish. And the city's peculiar weekly school schedule did make Decatur different. But that is not a reason for Decatur to have Saturday school in the first place.

Circuit-riding ministers needed Monday as a travel or rest day. No person who suggested this reason offered any evidence to support it. In telephone interviews, historians of the Presbyterian, Methodist, and Baptist faiths (see Interviews) express their puzzlement over just how such travel needs could affect a public school system. How many itinerant ministers would it have taken to cause the school board, the city commission, and the community to alter the school calendar?

Monday was an unsatisfactory school day. This rationale, suggested by school board chairman Dr. F.T. Hopkins after the 1922 vote, is neither profound, persuasive, nor convincing. Still, this is the only recorded reason given around the first public vote. Dr. Hopkins dropped that curious view five years later when he changed his position and voted for a Saturday weekly holiday.

It kept students from doing their homework on Sunday. This rationale was suggested by many interviewees. According to this view, closing school on Mondays helped to enforce observing the Sabbath because it removed an incentive for students to do their homework on Sunday night.

Many people in Decatur did honor the Lord's Day by not working, cooking, or even opening the Sunday newspaper. The Christian holy day was strictly observed. In addition, new cultural tensions seemed to threaten the Sabbath. For example, golf was becoming popular, especially on Sundays. The few people who owned cars increasingly went on Sunday drives; and as automobile ownership grew, Sunday driving flourished (Allen 1964, pp. 172, 294). Thus the devout in Decatur may have felt it necessary to protect the Sabbath by whatever means they could.

However, it is unclear why the devout in Decatur could not make their children do homework on Friday evening or Saturday. Again, in interviews with historians of Decatur's three major faiths — Presbyterian, Methodist, and Baptist — the historians denied that the established religious traditions would have affected a local public school system in such a way.

It kept Jews out of Decatur. Decatur had Saturday school for the covert purpose of keeping out Jews. This reason is most likely the real one for Decatur's unusual school schedule. My source for this judgment is the extensive oral history.

No written documents have been uncovered that record such a purpose; indeed, I would be astonished if there were such explicit material. Many policy discussions are never recorded. Especially in the first third of this century, politicians could debate and decide a policy in private. The official record shows only the action that was taken.

Yet despite the lack of written evidence, there is an oral record. In order to make sense of Decatur's insistence on having school on Saturdays, I interviewed a number of people who experienced and remembered Saturday school.

Among the many discussions and interviews I conducted, several stand out for their honesty and frankness. One such exchange took place in the Historic Court House, located on the Decatur town square, on 9 December 1997. The discussion took place during the 175th anniversary of the forming of DeKalb County.

Olive Morgan Dougherty, a seventh-generation DeKalb County resident, and I were both looking at a glass-encased exhibit on the court house's main floor. A black gentleman from Stone Mountain and a white county employee were with us when we discussed her experiences as a Decatur student.

Q. Did you attend school on Saturdays?

A. Yes, I went on Saturdays some of the years. I graduated in 1934.

Q. Why did Decatur have school on Saturday?

A. To keep out the Jews. . . .

Q. Ms. Morgan Dougherty, may I ask you a sensitive question?

A. Yes.

Q. Why did folks in Decatur want to keep the Jews out by having school on Saturday?

A. Bad Christians. (Dougherty, 9 December 1997)

Not only was Ms. Morgan Dougherty's mother a teacher, but her aunt was principal of Glennwood School, one of the oldest schools in Decatur. These family connections make her an impressive witness.

Very many interviewees have made extremely supportive comments during long-distance conversations similar to this brief and pointed exchange:

A. I have always heard we had Saturday School to keep out the Jews.

Q. How do you know?

A. I just know. I figured it out for myself. (Campbell, 3 January 1995)

Lifetime residents have reflected on my research question: "Why did Decatur have school on Saturday?" And whether in a small group sitting on a bench on historic East Court Square or individually over the telephone, many respondents — especially elderly women — have responded forthrightly. When I have asked why Decatur had Saturday school, several women have offered these typical brief answers: "We have always heard to keep out the Jewish." "It was the Jewish." "We didn't want Jews."

Respondents often associated a name with the action of approving Saturday as a school day. Invariably, a familiar name in Decatur and DeKalb County was mentioned: "Scott Candler didn't want Jews here."

I engaged a local mortician, Mr. Ralph Turner, in a typical conversation in front of the post office during my research phase.

Q. You went to school in Decatur, didn't you?
A. Yes, all my life.
Q. Did you go on Saturday?
A. Yes, I did.
Q. Why did you go on Saturday, if you know?
A. Everybody said, because we didn't want Jews in the schools.
Q. Where did you hear that?
A. Everywhere. (Turner, 11 April 1995)

Though the use of Saturday school to exclude Jews from Decatur seems to have been well known, Decatur residents also seem to have been reluctant to face this chapter in their history. For example, in a 1988 video recording of former Decatur mayor, Andy Robertson, he tells a friendly audience of old-timers at a DeKalb Historical Society program:

> Talk about being narrow-minded. I never went to school on Mondays in my life. I went on Saturdays. The obvious reason why was the Jewish Sabbath. They assumed if they had school on Saturday . . .

Then he lowers his eyes, shrugs his shoulders, and changes the subject. This recording was made more than 60 years after his own graduation from high school in 1923, and he still could hardly speak the truth (Robertson, *I Remember Hour*, 1988).

Frances Pauley, a former head of the Georgia Human Rights Commission and a longtime Decatur resident, had mentioned the same objective: to keep out the Jews. In fact, she was the person who first asked me if I knew about Decatur's history of Saturday School (Pauley, 19 December 1994).

Another woman with a rich local history, Lillian Salter, former secretary to the preeminent historian of Atlanta, Franklin Garrett, reflected on her own experience in the adjoining Druid Hills community around the Emory University campus. The details of that interview are included below. Her recorded experience shows a pattern of discrimination in both neighboring communities. Decatur's attitude toward Jews was reflected in the Emory community of DeKalb County.

Lillian Salter clearly remembered why the campus school at Emory University had Saturday classes: "The reason was we had some Jews in the school and we wanted to keep out any others" (Salter, 13 January 1995).

Former Congressman James A. Mackay, a highly regarded official and a conversationalist of known renown, said in a telephone interview: "No one ever said it right out, but when I put up a shingle and hung around the court house crowd, I'd hear everything that was true and some things that weren't. It just makes sense, especially with what Andy Robertson said" (Mackay, 7 March 1996).

The reason for Saturday School still touches every community in DeKalb County. In her interview, Emily Campbell Boland emphasized: "Our parents and ancestors kept folks from us. They kept us from learning about the world as it is. For that I am still upset" (Boland, 30 December 1994).

5

Decatur:
Homes, Schools, Churches,
and a Junkyard

When the first public schools were established in Decatur in 1902, the town had 1,400 residents. The town had electric lights but few other conveniences. Parks and streets were muddy, and there was no modern plumbing. There was a private academy for each sex.

A decade later, water and sewerage lines had been installed, sidewalks laid, streets paved, and a public school district established for white and black children. The U.S. census figures for Decatur for the first three decades tell part of the story.

1900	1910	1920	1930
1,418	2,466	6,150	13,276

Decatur's black population doubled from 1,266 in 1920 to 2,515 at the decade's end. Decatur maintained its native white/black ratio of approximately 80/20 throughout the decade, while the number of foreign-born whites who lived within its borders stayed below 125 persons throughout the first three decades (U.S. Census Bureau, 1900-1930).

The first public schools had about 430 students. By 1910, there were 587 students. In 1913, there were 615 white students and 139 black students. Two years later the town topped 3,500 including 820 pupils. By the end of World War I, the town's population exceeded 6,000, and the combined elementary and high school attendance was 1,296 (Board of Education, *Minutes*, 1902-1919).

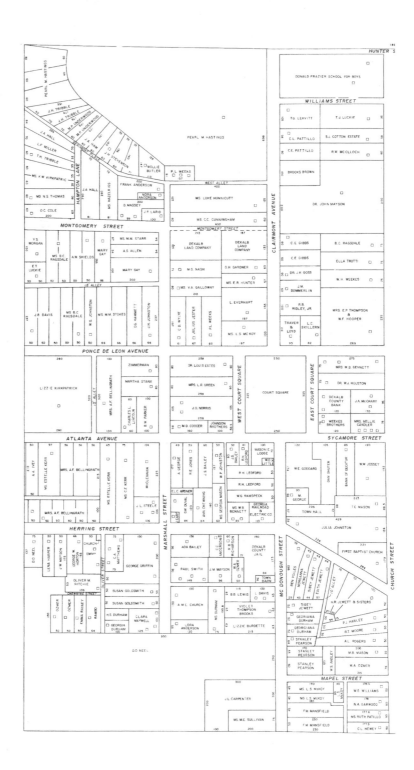

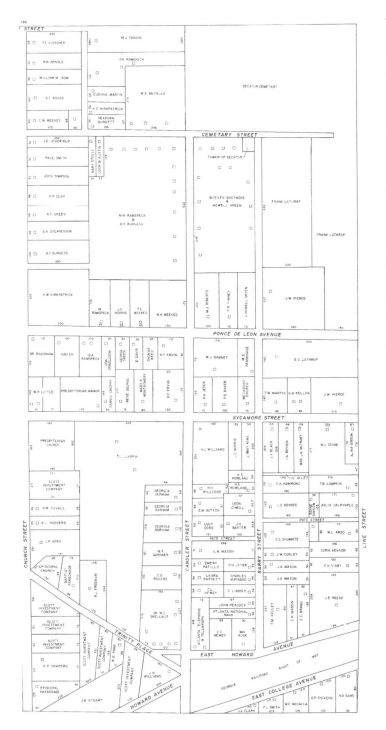

This map shows the corporate limits of the town of Decatur in 1912. Many of the major figures in the story of Decatur's school schedule lived just outside of the southern boundary in an area that did not become part of Decatur until the town expanded and became a city.

33

Decatur's form of government changed on 1 January 1921. The town was redesignated as a city, and the corresponding change in the form of government deeply divided the community. The political tensions were so great that the entire city commission resigned on 3 March 1922, and a new commission was elected on 7 April 1922 (City Commission, *Minutes*, January 1916 to 21 December 1923).

The new form of government, the new status as a city, and the new commissioners marked the beginning of Decatur's modern era and the meteoric rise to power of George Scott Candler. Candler became mayor in 1922 and served continuously until 1939, with only a one-year break in 1934. Candler's power continued to increase, and in the 1940s he became the sole county commissioner. One old saying was that whatever Scott Candler wanted politically, his friend and lawyer, John Wesley Weekes, could get done legally and — like to the divinity — in a six-day week.

Boosterism and strong political leadership paid off for Decatur. By 1928, Decatur had 550 business licenses. A sample of the businesses, published in the DeKalb *New Era* on 8 December 1927, gives a sense of the community: 7 barber shops, 9 dry clothing companies and pressing clubs, 5 shoe repair shops, 2 monument dealers and marble yards, 4 cafes and several lunch stands, 2 banks, 1 millinery shop, 5 ice and coal dealers, 3 transfer companies, 5 plumbing shops, 4 hardware stores, 1 blacksmith shop, 1 hotel (the Hotel Candler), 3 grain and feed stores, 10 drug stores, 1 lumber yard, 2 beauty parlors, and 1 grist mill. The newspaper story concluded on a wry note: "There are a number of physicians, lawyers, and dentists not subject to license."

There were many other businesses in Decatur, as well as organ grinders, "junk gatherers, by wagon or otherwise," lightning rod dealers, and other traveling salesmen (City Commission, *Minutes*, 4 January 1924 to 1 June 1928).

The city of Decatur engaged heavily in boosterism, as did many similar cities throughout the country in the 1920s. One element of Decatur's self-promotion that was less common was its boast that it was "different" from other cities, especially different from nearby Atlanta. One example of this sense of difference was quoted earlier, concerning Decatur's insistence on being different on the question of Sunday movies.

Though Decatur's belief in being different ran deep, that difference must be understood in terms of the bigotry and paranoia of the 1920s. People who were really different — southern Europeans and Russian Jews, for example — were not welcome. While Decatur celebrated its "difference," it was by no means a place open to real difference.

It also is important to see Decatur's sense of difference in terms of its neighboring city, Atlanta. By 1930 Atlanta had a population of 270,000, which included approximately 5,000 foreign-born whites and 90,000 blacks. The capital city had grown almost eight-fold since 1880 (U.S. Census Bureau, 1900-1930).

Atlanta had about 525 Jews in 1880, and this number grew proportionately to about 1,500 by 1916. However, in the next decade a phenomenal 700% growth occurred as the membership in Jewish congregations mushroomed to 11,000. In 1920 there were more Jewish congregants than all three of the Presbyterian bodies combined. After the Southern Baptist Convention, Negro Baptists, and the Methodist Episcopal Church South, came the 11,000 Jews in five congregations (Bureau of Census, *Religious Bodies*, 1926, p. 366).

From 1901 to 1922, the Industrial Removal Office (IRO) removed Jewish immigrants from New York City and sent them into smaller American cities where both jobs and Jewish communities existed. Atlanta received 654 Jews from the IRO between 1901 and 1915 (Rockaway 1993, p. 567).

The rest of the growth in Atlanta's Jewish population can be partially explained by the influx of Jews looking for work as bakers, butchers, cabinetmakers, laborers, peddlers, pressers, tailors, and tinsmiths. There also were Jewish bookkeepers, dentists, draughtsmen, glovemakers, milliners, Kosher butchers, and teachers who came to Atlanta looking for better lives.

This large influx of Eastern European Jews was concentrated almost entirely in Atlanta. In 1916 there were no recorded Jewish people in DeKalb County. Whether by design or deviousness, Decatur's actions kept almost all the Jews out of this town on the eastern border of Atlanta.

However, Jews who had lived in Atlanta for several generations, and who were somewhat assimilated, were moving north into Atlanta's Morningside neighborhood and the Druid Hills/ Emory University section of DeKalb County. The Druid Hills development bordered on Decatur.

In Decatur, a perverted group loyalty and hatred began to play itself out by the dominant white Protestant groups against anything seen as "un-American" (Allen 1964, p. 52).

The *Decatur, Georgia, City Directory 1928-29* included a category titled "Secret Societies," listed immediately after "Screens — Windows and Door." According to the directory, Decatur had five secret societies by 1928, including the IOOF and Rebekahs, which had their lodges at 119 E Court Square, and the Masons, which had three chapters located on the third floor of the Masonic Temple on the corner of Clairmont and East Ponce de Leon, including the Decatur Chapter 119, Order of the Eastern Star, Chapter 148, and Pythagoras Lodge No. 41.

An article in the DeKalb *New Era* (29 December 1921) mentions that the Pythagoras Lodge No. 41 F&AM was one of the oldest Masonic bodies in that area of Georgia. It had been organized in 1846, and in 1921 it had 416 members. The article also listed Scott Candler as a Past Master of that lodge.

Robert Ramspeck, the leather-lunged booster of Decatur who became a congressman, also was instrumental in the reconstitution of the Ku Klux Klan in Georgia. A handful of the senior residents that I interviewed mentioned seeing white robes in the closets of their friends or relatives (for example, McCurdy, 28 January 1998).

We need to remember that it was not only in Decatur that the robes of the Ku Klux Klan hung in the closets of prominent businessmen. All over America successful, middle-class, ambitious men — lawyers, doctors, ministers, and so forth — actively supported the Klan. Their common aim was resistance to change (Barry 1997, p. 154).

In some respects the Klan was a folk movement, not unlike populism. But it contained a heavy dose of paranoia. The Klan thrived on that old drama of "us" versus "them," where the role of the "them" could be cast as an absent Jewish boss or a newly arrived Catholic immigrant. A DeKalb County resident and Decatur graduate who was reluctant to be interviewed, and flatly refused to be identified, one day exploded with the reason for what was going on between Decatur and "the Jewish": "We hated them! Those sharpies! It wasn't their religion, it was *them*! They were sharpies."

The intolerance of many of Decatur's citizens allowed the City Commission, through its appointment power, and Mayor George S. Candler to exclude the Jews simply because they were different. However, Candler's bigotry was noted only in hushed tones. The late Lillian Salter's remark may help explain the attitude many had toward not only Candler's power but also his inhumanity in general when she said, "Where Scott Candler spit, no grass would grow." It was George Scott Candler's vote, control, and power over board members that helped keep Jews out of Decatur during the 1920s.

Located between Atlanta and Stone Mountain, Decatur was well within the Klan's epicenter. But Decatur did not indulge in such overt acts of ugliness and terror as the Atlanta pogrom of 1915 and the earlier race riot in 1906. These acts of violence had no place in Decatur. Instead, Decatur used a clever calendar, an undiscussed *sub rosa* mechanism, a silent deviousness through a device at once so subtle and yet so ingrained in the ways of the community that one former student of those times could honestly come forth with a rationale that seemed so plausible: "We went to school on Saturday because Superintendent Ferguson said so."

Decatur's intolerance was supported by its churches. The churches were particularly important in Decatur. In a special guest column, titled "Why I Live in Decatur," Reverend Adiel Jarrett Moncrief wrote that "As most of Decatur residents have their businesses in Atlanta, and also seek their diversion there, the churches are largely the centers of social contacts within the city" (DeKalb *New Era*, 8 December 1927). In that same article,

Moncrief explained that it was Decatur's homogeneousness that made the town a pleasant place to live: "The people in Decatur in unusually large proportions have common racial instincts and common historical traditions, and these things make cordial sympathies."

In the DeKalb *Wonder*, published monthly by the Decatur Chamber of Commerce, Robert Ramspeck wrote:

> Decatur has splendid churches. Today nine churches are within the city limits. They are all active and have a growing membership. They work in harmony, and the controlling influences of Decatur are the church, the school, and the home. Many good people are annually attracted to our city because of the distinctive atmosphere which exists here. Our people will permit nothing in Decatur that is harmful to our boys and girls. (1926)

But it was its schools that Decatur claimed as the first and finest fruits of a growing community. In his special guest column, "Why I Live in Decatur," A.J. Moncrief wrote that Decatur:

> has superior educational advantages, for there are few places where a home can be so situated that children may have access to good schools beginning with kindergarten and extending through college, university, and seminary, with excellent vocational and professional schools at hand so these children may remain at home throughout the entire period of their education. (DeKalb *New Era*, 8 December 1927)

The perception of superior schools rested partly on factual grounds and partly in the minds of Decaturites. Moncrief explained one part of this perception, saying:

> so I wish to point out some values that may not be as concrete as those mentioned but are even more to be desired. . . . The people of Decatur in unusually large portions have common racial instincts and common historical traditions, and these things make cordial sympathies. The community spirit of the city is an attractive asset. The moral tone of Decatur is high and its people are intelligently interested in spiritual and cultural values.

Apparently, Decatur's high moral tone and cultural values led its leaders to use the schools as a weapon against any Jews who might try to settle within the city's borders.

Interestingly, there was a Jewish family in Decatur, though other residents may not have known the family's true ethnic background. Sam Rittenbaum, his wife, Rose, and their daughters, Annie and Mollie, lived in Decatur at 241 Trinity Place. The Rittenbaums had come from Minsk.

After the father settled in the town, he brought his two daughters to Decatur. Shortly after the daughters arrived in the city, their father sat them down and started talking about living in Decatur. According to an interview with Mollie Rittenbaum Goldwasser, her father said: "Don't tell anyone you are Jewish. They don't allow Jews in Decatur" (Goldwasser, 14 February 1995).

When asked how her father had managed to accommodate living in Decatur, Goldwasser answered, "They thought he was Greek." Sam Rittenbaum's swarthy features helped him pretend to be from another culture. When pressed why her father had chosen to live in a town that did not want Jews, Mollie reflected that her father had wanted a small town because it was good for business. Also, his brothers were already in Atlanta, and he wanted to be on his own. She also remembered that her family did not know any German Jews, whom they called "rich Jews" (Goldwasser, 14 February 1995).

Sam Rittenbaum collected and peddled bottles, junk, and rags on a horse and wagon. The Hotel Candler and Sam Rittenbaum are the only two businesses identified by name in the 1928 Decatur City Directory. Neither documents nor interviews explain this anomaly. Sam Rittenbaum lived from 1884 until 1939 and was buried in Greenwood cemetery in Atlanta.

Mollie had come from Minsk to Decatur in 1922 and had been put into third grade; Annie, the older daughter, was in the fifth grade. The sisters owned only four dresses.

In the late 1920s, Decatur boys rode the trolley to Atlanta for a nickel, purchased a quarter-pound of chocolate candy for a dime, and then went to Decatur Days on Mondays at the newly opened movies. The Decatur girls went into Atlanta to shop at Rich's. However, Mollie Rittenbaum rode the streetcar to work at a retail store on Decatur Street in Atlanta. Then she came back to her home town and picked cotton. Despite the Klan's stereotype of immigrants being shiftless, Mollie actually worked more than did her native-born classmates (Goldwasser, 14 February 1995).

Annie Rittenbaum graduated in 1930, and Mollie graduated two years later in 1932. Symbolically, Mollie's graduation marks the end of the era of Saturday school. The commencement exercises for Decatur High School were held on Sunday, 5 June 1932, at 11:00 a.m. in the high school auditorium. The program followed the traditional format for the "Order of Worship." Students and parents sang two hymns, "All Hail the Power" and "Holy, Holy, Holy," while Reverend A.B. Couch delivered the sermon, "A Life's Right to Exist" (Goldwasser, *Memorabilia*, 14 February 1995).

The graduation ceremony concluded on Monday, June 6, at 8:00 p.m. in the Agnes Scott Auditorium. Dr. A.J. Moncrief gave both the invocation and benediction. Rev. Wallace Alston delivered the baccalaureate address, while board of education member C.D. McKinney handed out the 92 diplomas (Goldwasser, *Memorabilia*, 14 February 1995).

To mark her graduation from the school system, which had silently yet effectively worked to exclude other Jewish children, this diminutive Russian Jewish girl had followed all the acceptable rituals. She had a Gothic-lettered graduation card: "Miss Mollie M. Rittenbaum." She and Eva Hazelrig donated their entertaining abilities to the "Burley Bodenhamers," as a part of the Class of 1932 "Last Will and Testament." She had participated in having her yearbook signed with the usual sentimental wishes, including this one from Mrs. C. Folger: "May your life be bright and skinny, and your husband fat and funny." Her remembrance book, with a beautiful floral design in the center of each page, had statements from friends, adults, and well-wishers written in a pie-shaped fashion, radiating from a center flower: "May your success start from this day on." "Hope you will always enjoy life with others as I have with you." "You are a very funny little girl, and I like you lots. Don't forget me after this year 'cause I'll always remember you. Lots of love" (Goldwasser, *Memorabilia*, 14 February 1995).

Mollie Rittenbaum Goldwasser did not suspect that the Saturday school she attended as a child was an exclusionary device, a peculiar practice in Decatur. While growing up, she just tended to her own business, as did so many youngsters of that era. When she learned about the possible reason for a Monday holiday, she was genuinely shocked and pressed me to find the details and the truths in her own public school history.

Decatur had become different because of the Rittenbaums. Their entrepreneurial spirit meant that the city would be described as a place of homes, schools, churches, and a junkyard.

6

A Parallel Case

While the practice of Saturday school in Decatur was peculiar, it was not unique. A school district associated with nearby Emory College adopted a similar practice in 1923.

When Emory College moved from Oxford, Georgia, to Atlanta in 1919, faculty members wanted a school for their children. Poor roads, prejudgments about existing schools, and sentiment favoring a university school led to temporary quarters in the chapel for 43 students.

Four years later, in 1923, the L.C. Fishburne Building was built at Emory University. It housed the first unit of Emory's Teachers College and an elementary and high school for children of the faculty and children from the Emory and Druid Hills neighborhoods (English 1966, p. 29). In 1927 a special school district was created for Fishburne, bounded partly by Decatur on the south and carved out of three other districts. W.D. Thomson, Walter Candler, and Fred C. Mason were chosen as trustees for three-, two-, and one-year terms, respectively. Walter Candler was the second cousin of George Scott Candler.

The Fishburne building was an architectural beauty. It had two floors, a sloping roof, block marble walls, and two round-urn chimneys. It had many paneled windows, which, on the eastern side, were fitted with blinds to keep out the sun. The Fishburne School operated until 1929, when the Druid Hills High School opened. And during the six years in which the school was located in the Fishburne Building, it also had Saturday classes and Monday holidays.

Among those graduates of the Fishburne School who discussed its history with me, there were a local educator who became a DeKalb County principal, an important local building contractor, and an assistant to Atlanta's most famous historian. These three alumni of Fishburne illustrate in their reflections the difficulties encountered, both in finding the facts of and telling the story behind Saturday School in Decatur.

For example, the retired principal remembered school on Saturday well enough, yet he could not recall anything about the reasons for this unusual approach to the weekly schedule. The contractor, Clyde Shepherd, recalled an unfinished dirt floor, lunch boxes with sandwiches, and dodge ball during recess. He remembered classmates' names, house locations of the lawyer for Coca Cola, and the tuition his father paid during his five years of attendance. He also recollected his Tuesday through Saturday classes. Yet he vehemently denied they were held for any reason connected with excluding Jewish people. Mr. Shepherd believed that his father, who was highly involved in local matters, would have mentioned such a fact.

> I never heard about keeping out the Jews. We had no problem with the Jewish. No situation. We also thought we had Saturday school because Emory and the bishops were very religious. I knew lots of the families of the Jewish and still do. We never had a problem. (Shepherd, 1 April 1998)

On the other hand, the late Mrs. Lillian Salter, a former secretary-assistant to the preeminent Atlanta historian, Franklin Garrett, recalled her school days in the same detail and with a completely different insight. While researching the facts of this book, my wife and I met with Franklin Garrett, author of *Atlanta and Its Environs*. Garrett graciously agreed to receive us at his office at the Atlanta Historical Society; but no sooner had we begun the interview than a slightly stooped, diminutive woman started working on papers arranged behind his desk. Although she certainly knew her way around the room, I was a bit annoyed because she was distracting us during our conversation with this important figure.

Mr. Garrett said he knew nothing whatever about Saturday School, that he could remember nothing at all associated with Decatur's peculiar practice; yet he did offer an insight into the times. He mentioned that he recalled a ditty that children sang during his childhood. I leaped to the conclusion that he was thinking of "Red Rover" or some such typical rhyme; it was with total astonishment that I heard the following:

> Jew boy, Jew boy,
> Where'd you get those socks?
> Wholesale, retail?
> Twenty cents a box?
> Jew boy, Jew boy,
> Where'd you get those socks?
> (Garrett, 13 January 1995)

Obviously, the advantages of buying at wholesale were the least important implications of this ditty. As the interview progressed, Garrett said he knew of a helpful book and excused himself to try and find it. As he was going out the door, the elderly lady, Mrs. Lillian Salter, who had come in and out of the room incessantly, asked her employer's permission to speak. And the impact of her unsolicited, voluntary statement is still with me.

"I went to Fishburne school on Saturdays," she said. Those seven words were the author's first inkling of the fact that a nearby school, associated with Emory University and located two miles from Decatur, had seen fit to copy this peculiar practice.

When Ms. Salter came forward with the reason for Saturday school, our research with the noted historian almost came to a halt. As we listened intently to her every word, this refined, respectful woman spoke in the clearest terms.

> Everyone knew that we had millionaires' children in the school and that we also had several Jewish students. The area of Druid Hills was often called "Jewid Hills." We had Saturday school so we wouldn't have more Jews in our school. (Salter, 13 January 1995)

45

During a subsequent phone call, Mrs. Salter discussed in greater detail her fondness for those elementary school days. "I had a crush on a first-grader who was Jewish," she admitted. She had quizzed her mother about her first-grade love and his attendance at church; and her mother, in turn, had clarified the differences of faith, doctrine, and places and times of worship. And now, many years later, Mrs. Salter was making clear the depth and permanence of her personal understanding of Fishburne's history by telling us of that first love in the quiet, dignified tones of her measured whisper (Salter, 13 April 1995).

Later she discussed the reason for Saturday School with three of her contemporary women friends at a lunch. When last we spoke on the phone before her death, she confirmed that the three not only remembered, but agreed on, the reason for Saturday classes at the Fishburne school. Saturday was scheduled as a school day in order to keep Jewish boys and girls out of Emory College's Fishburne School.

7

What's True? Who Cares?

When people asked me questions during the writing of this monograph, I took special note. For example, one person plaintively queried me: "Are you writing about your own hometown?" "Where did this come from?" "What difference does it make?" The answers to those questions, for me, seem straightforward. Not only did I write a story about my current hometown, but I hope that many people will write more complete histories about the public schools in their hometowns. The history of American public education should be told as completely as possible, warts and all. Only then will we understand how our current institutions have come to be and where they may be going. Nor do these histories need to be written by professional historians. Most people in this country have attended public schools; thus many important histories wait to be told.

While several men from Decatur discussed Saturday school with me, we often would focus on a single point or historical fact, such as the tie vote in 1922. Then one of the elderly individuals would ask me two questions, usually phrased as a couplet: "So what? Who cares?" These two questions have not haunted me, but they have caused me to reflect on the reasons I worked on this monograph.

Why does a story from the 1920s mean anything in the last years of the millennium? The answer, of course, is that history is important because, without a knowledge of history, we cannot truly understand the present. Without understanding, we repeat the mistakes of the past. Without truth, we cannot be free.

To understand the truth about Decatur and Saturday school, the reader needs to consider not only the facts but also the times in which they occurred. Those times included certain beliefs, assumptions, and customs that are different than those held today. However, they also included beliefs that still are widespread. We may not be as different from our forefathers as we try to believe.

We still make up stories to disguise the past. I am not discounting the honesty and integrity of those who suggested that it was the Monday washday, agricultural needs, college travel, differences in Decatur's way of life, a rest day for ministers, an unsatisfactory day for learning, or protecting the Sabbath from homework that led to Decatur holding classes on Saturday. I am quite certain that these reasons are truly believed by the honest, church-going, Decatur residents who propounded them. But I believe they are just excuses that the people in the 1920s told themselves to disguise the real reason for Saturday school.

Of course, there remains the possibility that the reason for a Monday holiday changed over time, that the community established Saturday school for religious reasons that changed as the country became more secular during the 1920s. But I have found no evidence, either written or oral, to support this view.

Decatur had effectively transmitted the silent message: "Jewish: Keep Out." Decatur simply built an invisible wall for the specific purpose of keeping out "the Jewish," and it did so under the pretext of the Christian religion. There is a well-known name for such practices: *Judenrein*, which means "cleansed of Jews." Today there still are attempts to exclude those who are different, and the pretexts for those attempts take a variety of forms.

I began my research because a woman who lived in the 1920s shared her recollection about Decatur's way of life. And she did that because she knew of my love for education. From that one statement, I spent three years researching the facts and thinking about meanings of the story.

Many of the men I interviewed were hesitant to discuss the events of those earlier days. The women were more forthright, more accurate in their recollections, and much more willing to share their stories. But both men and women encouraged me because they cared. And as more of the story became known, I was surprised by the many people, both young and old, who cared about what had been done in their community and why it had become the way it is now.

Saturday school is an unusual example of anti-Semitic behavior. Those in power used a clever manipulation of the school calendar to exclude those who were somehow different. Elected and appointed officials were using their power to decide who would be accepted as a citizen, and their policies affected Decatur long after the peculiar practice was ended. At the writing of this book, in late 1998, fewer than 20 Jewish families own homes in Decatur. It is not by accident that this is so.

The intentions behind public policy must be studied. To this day, few citizens attend the meetings of school boards, though these bodies decide vital public policies. The story of Saturday school illustrates the gap between what we say and what we do. It also should teach us about the subtle ways in which our schools can exclude people. We need to know the truth, and we need to care.

Appendix

Research

For five days between 20 and 24 February 1995, my wife, Lynne, who is a writer, and I researched superintendent and board of education annual reports at the Monroe C. Gutman Library at the Graduate School of Education of Harvard University. These Public School Reports in the Gutman Library's special collection were available to us under the supervision of the special collections librarian.

Since the documents were very fragile, we donned white gloves and masks during our daily, seven-hour research sessions. We examined more than 1,500 documents, including at least 30 annual reports from districts in each of the continental 48 states, from urban district reports, and from state and federal departments of education materials. The annual reports we reviewed from 1900-1935 often listed starting days and dates, daily schedules, weekly class arrangements, holiday periods, policies on school calendars, and the exact arrangement of daily lessons under chapters called "Rules and Regulations." For example, the West Allis Public Schools of Wisconsin showed a monthly, weekly, and yearly calendar of 200 days on one page for the year 1909-1910. Each week was a Monday-Friday calendar. The Greenville, Alabama, Public School 1901-02 Report stated General Rule #1:

> The school year shall begin on the first Monday in September and shall consist of nine scholastic months of four weeks each. (*Public School Reports*, 1900-1935)

The 1928 Rules and Regulations for the white and colored schools of Rome, Georgia, listed Article 2, "School Year," Item #1:

> The fall term shall begin on Thursday following the first Monday in September, and shall continue for thirty-six weeks of school work from the following Monday. (*Public School Reports*, 1900-1935)

51

Lynne Keating wears a mask and gloves to avoid damaging old documents at the Monroe C. Gutman Library at the Graduate School of Education of Harvard University as she helps conduct research on Saturday school in Decatur, Georgia.

In addition to reading these hundreds of documents, we took notes or duplicated school rules and calendars from at least three districts in each of 48 states, and these have been saved in our research files. We did not find in these records one other example of a school district or system with a Tuesday-Saturday class calendar. Not one.

Nor did we find anything in any state department of education material, federal directory, or report from a large urban area that even hinted at a variation of the standard Monday-Friday schedule. We also conducted database searches and questioned education historians without finding school systems with a schedule like that in Decatur.

However, we did find one isolated school in Palmyra, Virginia, that held school on Saturday. A single sentence on page 12 of the

1912-1913 report of Palmyra Normal High School stated: "The school week is from Tuesday to Saturday inclusive" (*Public School Reports*, 1900-1935). Naturally this sentence intrigued us.

Following the discovery of that school, I contacted Minnie Lee McGehee, co-author of a monograph in the *Bulletin of the Fluvanna County Historical Society* on the history of the schools in that area. She sent us a copy of her monograph, which included this statement:

> The 1906-7 session was for thirty-two weeks and students had six 30-minute recitations every day, Tuesday through Saturday. Monday was 'court day' at the county seat and no school was held; this schedule continued for many years. (McGehee and Bearr 1987, p. 41)

McGehee later sent a letter (pers. comm. 1 March 1995), which was even more detailed:

> I have interviewed many people who attended the Palmyra High School/Palmyra Normal School. Each told me classes were held on Tuesday through Saturday, because Monday was Court Day and the pupils used the Court Green as a playground. The school stood just behind the Court Green and beside the Palmyra Methodist Church. The church and the Court House both had protective shutters which were closed when the buildings were not in use to protect the windows from the balls and other sports items.

Apparently, the children's shouting distracted the judges, so the schedule was changed so no school was held on Monday. Thus school on Saturday made sense in Fluvanna County for the practical reason of keeping the area quiet during court day.

Interviews

The following interviews are listed by individual, place, and date.

Boland, Emily Campbell. Decatur. 30 December 1994.
Calloway, Lula. Decatur. 6 September 1997.

Dougherty, Olive Morgan. Decatur. 9 December 1997.

Flynt, Frances Treadwell. Decatur. 8 November 1997.

Garrett, Franklin. Atlanta. 13 January 1995.

Goldwasser, Mollie Rittenbaum. Marietta, Georgia. 14 February 1995.

Greene, Graham. Decatur. 20 January 1995.

McCurdy, Walter, Jr. Decatur. 28 January 1998.

McKinney, Charles D. Decatur. 17 January 1995.

Pauley, Frances Freeborn. Decatur. 19 December 1994.

Ridley, John. Decatur. 11 April 1995.

Salter, Lillian. Atlanta. 13 January 1995.

Shepherd, Clyde. Decatur. 1 April 1998.

Turner, Ralph. Decatur. 11 April 1995.

Wilkins, Commander Bennie. Decatur. 2 February 1995.

Williams, Wheat, Jr. Decatur. 4 February 1995.

The following local and long-distance telephone conversations are listed by individual and date.

Bynum, William. 31 July 1998.

Campbell, William B. 3 January 1995.

Clarke, Erskine. 31 July 1998.

Egerton, John. 24 April 1995.

Holifield, Brooks. 18 July 1995.

Honniker, Leila. 4 February 1996.

Huser, Fred. 15 March 1995.

Link, Arthur. 24 March 1995.

Mackay, James. 7 March 1996.

McGehee, Minnie Lee. 27 February 1995.

Robertson, Andrew. 29 November 1994.

Ross, Kenneth. 15 March 1995; 31 July 1998.

Salter, Lillian. 13 April 1995.

Sams, Eileen Dodd. 28 January 1998.

Sams, Hansford. 20 January 1995.

Smylie, James. 31 July 1998.

Thompson, Elizabeth. 17 January 1998.

Williams, Michael. 19 July 1995.

Wittenstein, Charles. 4 January 1995.

Other

Atlanta Constitution. 2 March 1927.

Decatur Board of Education. *Minutes.* 1902-07; 1908-1910; 1910-1915; 1915-1919; 1920-1929; 1930-1932.

Decatur Chamber of Commerce. *DeKalb Wonder.* 1926.

Decatur City Commission. *Minutes.* 1882-1904; 6 December 1904 to 19 November 1911; 1 January 1912 to 31 December 1915; 3 January 1916 to 21 December 1923; 4 January 1924 to 1 June 1928; 15 June 1928 to 3 January 1936.

Decatur Girls' High School. *Stylus.* 1933.

Decatur High School. *Caveal Emptor: Annals of Decatur High School, 1922-1931.*

DeKalb *New Era.* November 1921; August 1922; February, March, and December 1927.

Goldwasser, Mollie Rittenbaum. Memorabilia. Shared at interview, 14 February 1995.

Gutman Library, Harvard University. *Public School Reports.* Selected annual reports from 48 states and municipalities, surveyed 1900-1935.

Holderman, Julius, publ. *Decatur, Georgia, City Directory 1928-29.*

Superior Court of Fulton County, Georgia. *Charter of the Knights of the Ku Klux Klan.* 1916.

Chronology

1902

Jan. 6   Decatur schools open on Monday for four-month term.

Sept. 2   Board of education begins school on Tuesday for a nine-month school year.

1903

Aug. 31   School opens Monday for fall term.

1904-21

Board of education submits annual reports to city commission showing that all terms and vacation reopenings begin on Tuesdays.

1921

Nov. 21　Superintendent Glausier suggests changing weekly holiday from Monday to Saturday. Mr. McKinney moves this change be made effective beginning of spring term. Motion tabled.

1922

Aug. 29　Candler moves and Dr. Sledd seconds to keep Monday holiday. Vote ties. Chairman Hopkins casts deciding vote to keep Monday holiday.

1927

Feb. 8　Petitioners request board to change the school holiday from Monday to Saturday. Mrs. Hoke convinces board to vote at next meeting. Candler absent. Dr. Hopkins moves and board agrees to instruct superintendent Ferguson to send "colorless questionnaire" to parents.

Mar. 2　Superintendent mails surveys to white families. Parent-teacher groups in Decatur, represented by Mr. Howard, move to change holiday.

Mar. 8　Board discusses survey results of white parents favoring change. McKinney demands roll call vote for first time in Decatur history. Tie vote. The holiday remains Monday.

Mar. 18　Mrs. Hoke resigns with nine months remaining in her term. City Commission appoints Mrs. Howard to fill unexpired term of Mrs. Hoke.

1932

May 3　Mrs. Howard moves weekly holiday change from Monday to Saturday. Motion carries.

Jun. 4　School closes on Saturday for last time.

Bibliography

Allen, Frederick Lewis. *Only Yesterday*. New York: Harper & Rov
  Perennial Library, 1964.

Allen, Frederick Lewis. *Since Yesterday*. New York: Harper & Ro'
  Perennial Library, 1986.

Antin, Mary. *The Promised Land*. Princeton, N.J.: Princeton Universi
  Press, 1969.

Barry, John M. *Rising Tide: The Great Mississippi Flood of 1927 a
  How It Changed America*. New York: Simon and Schuster, 1997.

Bettmann, Otto L. *The Good Old Days: They Were Terrible*. New Yo
  Random House, 1974.

Blumberg, Janice Rothschild. *As But a Day*. Atlanta: Hebrew Bene'
  lent Congregation, 1987.

Butchart, Renald E. *Local Schools*. Nashville: American Associat
  for State and Local History, 1986.

Cash, W.J. *The Mind of the South*. New York: Knopf, 1941.

Clarke, Caroline McKinney. *The Story of Decatur 1823-1899*. Atla
  Higgins-McArthur/Longino & Porter, 1973.

Coulter, E. Merton. *Georgia: A Short History*. Chapel Hill: Univer
  of North Carolina Press, 1960.

Cremin, Lawrence A. *American Education: The Metropolitan Exp
  ence, 1876-1980*. New York: Harper & Row, 1988.

Dixon, Thomas, Jr. *The Clansman*. Lexington: University Press of I
  tucky, 1970.

Ecke, Melvin W. *From Ivy Street to Kennedy Center*. Atlanta: Atl
  Board of Education, 1972.

English, Thomas H. *Emory University 1915-1965*. Atlanta: Er
  University, 1966.

Felton, Mrs. William H. *My Memoirs of Georgia Politics*. Atlanta
  dex Printing Company, 1911.

Fogelson, Robert M., and Rubenstein, Richard E., eds. *Mass Vio'
  in America, Hearings on the Ku Klux Klan 1921*. New York:
  Press and the New York Times, 1969.

Garrett, Franklin M. *Atlanta and Environs*. vol. 2. New York: I
  Historical, 1954.

Goldstein, Judith S. *Crossing Lines*. New York: William Morrow and Company, 1992.

Grant, Donald. *The Way It Was in the South*. New York: Carse, 1993.

Hobson, Archie, ed. *Remembering America*. New York: Columbia University Press, 1985.

Howe, Irving. *World of Our Fathers*. New York: Simon and Schuster, 1976.

Joiner, Oscar, H., ed. *A History of Public Education in Georgia 1734-1976*. Columbia, S.C.: R.L. Bryan, 1979.

Kuhn, Clifford M.; Joye, Harlon E; and West, Bernard E. *Living Atlanta: An Oral History of the City, 1914-1948*. Athens: University of Georgia Press, 1990.

Kutler, Stanley I. *Looking for America: Vol. II, Since 1865*. New York: W.W. Norton, 1976.

Loewen, James W. *Lies My Teacher Taught Me*. New York: New Press, 1995.

McGehee, Minnie Lee, and Bearr, David W.C. *The Connecting Link*. Bulletin of the Fluvanna County Historical Society no. 43. Palmyra, Va.: Fluvanna County Historical Society, 1987.

Mowry, George E., ed. *The Twenties*. Englewood Cliffs, N.J.: Prentice-Hall, 1963.

Price, Vivian. The History of DeKalb County, Georgia, 1822-1900. Fernandina Beach, Fla.: Wolfe, 1997.

Robertson, Andrew. "I Remember Hour." Videotape. DeKalb County, Georgia, Historical Society, February 1988.

Rockaway, Robert A. " 'It's Hard Living in Atlanta': The Contrasting Views of Two Jewish Immigrants, 1905-1906." *Georgia Historical Quarterly* 3 (Fall 1993): 566-76.

Writers' Program of the Works Progress Administration in the State of Georgia. *Georgia: The WPA Guide to Its Towns and Countryside*. Athens: University of Georgia Press, 1940.

About the Author

Tom Keating was born in 1941 in Bradford, Pennsylvania. He graduated from Middlebury College in 1963 with a B.A. in political science. Following theological training at St. Meinrad, Indiana, he received an M.A. and Ph.D. in education policy and politics from Claremont Graduate School in California.

Keating taught in public and private schools in Jacksonville, Florida; Atlanta, Georgia; and Pomona, California. He was a college instructor at Atlanta University and in the State University Systems of Georgia and California. Keating received a Ford Fellowship in Education, allowing him to work for a year on the staff of the Illinois House Speaker.

His career includes 18 years as a self-employed educator, during which time he has served individual, institutional, and organizational clients, including the Atlanta Board of Education, where his tenure as governmental liaison for a school system was the longest in Georgia history.

Keating is the author *U.S. Department of Education: Legislative History and Reference Book* and *The Missing Policies and Politics of the Georgia Dropout Crisis*. He has written several articles for the *American School Board Journal*, including "Democracy Up Close" and "Let Your School Board Be a Lesson." He has successfully completed 26 grant proposals, which have funded projects in the areas of dropout prevention, rural health, public school restrooms, and environmental projects.

Keating's civic and professional commitment entails service as a former member of the Decatur Board of Education and as a frequent presenter during Education Week at the Chautauqua Institution. In order to stay close to young people, he presents dramatic performances to children and slide travelogues for families on his adventures with the 17 different kinds of penguins.

Tom and Lynne, his wife, are the parents of Jeffrey and Stephanie, both creative individuals. The Keatings have lived in Decatur, Georgia, for 20 years.